HILL COUNTRY WISDOM
A Cup of Coffee and a Chat with Doc

HEBREWS

Disk Sisk

Bold Vision Books
P. O. Box 2011
Friendswood, Texas 77549

Copyright 2013 ©Dick Sisk

Library of Congress Control Number: 2013937265
ISBN No. 978-0-9853563-8-5

Printed in the U.S.A.

BVB - Bold Vision Books
PO Box 2011
Friendswood, Texas 77549
Cover Photo: Hondo Creek, Tarpley, Texas

All Scripture quotations, unless otherwise indicated, are taken from the Holy Bible, New International Version®, NIV®. Copyright © 1973, 1978, 1984, 2011 by Biblica, Inc.™ Used by permission of Zondervan. All rights reserved worldwide. www.zondervan.com The "NIV" and "New International Version" are trademarks registered in the United States Patent and Trademark Office by Biblica, Inc.™
Scripture quotations marked "KJV" are taken from the Holy Bible, King James Version, Cambridge, 1769.

All rights reserved. No part of this publication may be reproduced, stored in a retrieval system, or transmitted in any form or by any means—electronic, mechanical, photocopy, recording, or any other—except for brief quotations in printed reviews, without the prior permission of the publisher. Requests for information or permissions should be addressed to Bold Vision Books, PO Box 2011, Friendswood, Texas 77549

DEDICATION

To those who have sustained my life,
encouraged me, and prayed for me the most: my
girls. My wife and sunshine of my life, Barbara,
and my daughters, of whom I am so proud,
Christy, Lisa, Becca, and Liz.

A cup of coffee and
a chat with a friend is
happiness tasted and
time well spent.

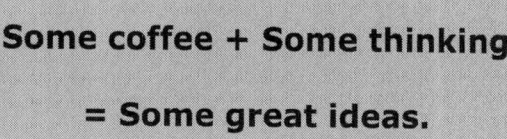

FOREWORD

I don't care who you are, you need a quiet time, a devotional, a first cup of God's Word to you every morning—or whenever you and the Lord have your time together.

My friend of 25 years plus, Dick Sisk, has always had a "sensible and sacred" word for his church and friends. Doc is a salt-of-the-earth preacher, teacher, and author who knows how to "get to ya" and "cut to the chase." Now he's done it while you have your first cup of java for the day.

I love how he has taken us through Hebrews for our "Java with Jesus" experience. This is good stuff! You will get the point and the message with each passage. Concise and concentrated.

How Doc does it I don't know - but with his years of being in the trenches, he has some wonderful words of wisdom. So, get a 2nd cup of coffee - or latte - whatever - and feed on God's Word and wisdom from Doc's words "fitly spoken" for such a time as this.

May the Lord Jesus bless you as you benefit from Hebrews and the Texas brew from a Texas pastor who has prepared you a cup that will give you the boost you need for today. And then, he will have another cup of God's truth for you tomorrow in the next devotional.

Blessings,
Dr. Dennis Swanberg
America's Minister of Encouragement
www.dennisswanberg.com

ACKNOWLEDGMENTS

I would like to acknowledge those who have given me the most encouragement in this project.

Thanks to those who first followed the writing of these thoughts and encouraged me to print them.

Thanks to the churches that have allowed me to learn and grow by serving as their pastor through the years, especially to my present church, Tarpley Baptist Church.

And finally thanks to Karen and George Porter and Bold Vision Books for their encouragement, guidance, suggestions, and belief in this project.

Legend has it that a 9th century Ethiopian shepherd discovered coffee by accident when he noticed how his goats danced and became frisky after eating the berries

INTRODUCTION

One of the most pleasant times of each day is spending time with my wife, Barbara, as we have our first cup of coffee in the morning. After we "wake" up with coffee, we both talk and listen to each other, and then pray together. During the spring, summer, and fall, the setting for these early mornings is on the porch of The Creek House, our home. The Creek House is also a Bed and Breakfast that we operate, at no charge, for pastors, missionaries, and Christian workers.

On many of the mornings, after our prayer time, Barbara starts her day and I remain on the porch, reading the Word, and thinking about its implications in my life. Wanting to clarify the thoughts, I began to write them and then posted the words on Facebook. I decided if I was going to participate in the Facebook phenomenon, then I would try to do something constructive. This book is the result of those early morning times in the Word and reflects what I learned from Hebrews.

In my mind, I pictured one or more of my friends sitting there on the porch with me, a cup of steaming coffee in hand, getting the day started off right as we discussed these thoughts.

Several years ago, the kids at church began calling me Doc. When our grandkids came along, they picked it up and we became Doc and Ba. So grab a cup and have a chat with Doc. I pray these thoughts on Hebrews will encourage.

--Doc

1

In the past God spoke to our ancestors through the prophets at many times and in various ways, but in these last days he has spoken to us by his Son, whom he appointed heir of all things, and through whom also he made the universe.
Hebrews 1:1–2

There is no one like Jesus. Although most of us would probably agree and say we believe Jesus is unique and above all, we don't act as if we are certain. The book of Hebrews was written to Hellenistic Jews. These Jews were most likely a displaced group living in Greece. Missionaries had reached them by this time and a small group of Jews had been converted. They were still holding to some of the rituals of the Old Testament.

The writer of Hebrews made the link between the old and the new, while showing how Christ had fulfilled the prophecies of the old. The recipients of the letter were about to undergo terrific persecution. Beginning with Nero's persecution in AD 64, these believers were tortured in unbelievable ways, including beheading and burning at the stake. Through the Holy Spirit's inspiration, the author warned them to focus on Christ, rather than drift back into Judaism.

To focus or to concentrate on Jesus means that a

person looks to Jesus and Jesus alone for his or her salvation, guidance, and wisdom, rather than trusting in works, or traditions, or church. Exercising faith in Christ and Christ alone means a person is not self-sufficient or dependent upon anyone other than Christ to solve problems or to get him or her through the rough times of life. It is a practical "looking unto Jesus, the author and finisher of our faith" (Hebrews 12:2). Even in difficult, sad, scary times, we focus on Him because there's no one like Him.

Like the Hebrews, we are on the verge of unprecedented times in our nation and world. The evening news reports wars, disturbances, national threats, storms, economic downturns, and joblessness. Yet when we focus on Christ, we are not afraid of the weather or dictators or political situations.

To focus on Christ, read His Word, pray, and put your confidence in Him. He is the only God, the only Creator, the only Savior; focus on Him.

Have a "focused on Him" day today.

2

In the past God spoke to our ancestors through the prophets at many times and in various ways, but in these last days he has spoken to us by his Son, whom he appointed heir of all things, and through whom also he made the universe.

Hebrews 1:1–2

The words of verses one and two remind how God's last word came to us. "but in these last days He has spoken to us by his Son."

We use the term, "having the last word" to mean that the discussion is over and so is the debate. Good conversation and debate are stimulating, healthy, and interesting, but sometimes the exchange can get heated or unpleasant. Then we want to be done with the argument.

When Hebrews said God has spoken in these last days "by His Son," it means, no matter how God has spoken in the past, His final way of revealing Himself to us is through His Son. Therefore, we need to pay close attention to Christ. What is He saying to us through His Word on a daily basis? You can get the last word by reading what Jesus said and examining His actions during His three years of ministry. He is the latest news, the final note, the crescendo. You can hear God by hearing Jesus.

Hear "the last word" today.

3

In the past God spoke to our ancestors through the prophets at many times and in various ways, but in these last days he has spoken to us by his Son, whom he appointed heir of all things, and through whom also he made the universe.
Hebrews 1:1–2

There is no one like Jesus. In the first four verses of Hebrews, there are seven statements to show how He is unlike any other. First of all, in verse two, we learn what makes Christ unique. He is "appointed heir of all things." The term "heir" describes what a father has left to his son.

Since, through Adam, we, as his sons, inherited a fallen nature and the resulting death sentence; we are said to be "Adam's heirs." When Adam fell, he lost the unbroken relationship with God—the gift from the Father in the Garden. It was "Paradise Lost."

When Jesus came in His humanity, and died on the cross for us, He regained everything Adam lost. He mended the relationship between the Father and us. He is an heir of the Father and we are heirs too. Paul said we are "joint heirs" with Christ. (See Romans 8:13-14). We share in the inheritance. Only a child of

God qualifies for the inheritance. Don't show up at the reading of the will and try to claim something that is not yours. But if you are His child, the inheritance is all yours too.

Have a "joint heir" day today.

4

In the past God spoke to our ancestors through the prophets at many times and in various ways, but in these last days he has spoken to us by his Son, whom he appointed heir of all things, and through whom also he made the universe.
Hebrews 1:1–2

Good morning. Hope your coffee tastes as good as mine this morning. It's cool here in the Hill Country of Texas.

Have I told you that there is no one like Jesus? We've learned He is the "heir of all things," but there are six more statements about His uniqueness. Next, He is Creator God—"through whom also He made the universe." The word universe used in these verses means the whole universe of both time and space. God made it all through Jesus--"all things were made by Him and without Him nothing was made."

He was with God in the beginning, and He was God in the beginning. (See John 1:1-3.) According to the Psalms, He spoke the world into existence. From the tiniest creature to the most magnificent mountains, He is the architect and the inventor.

Jesus is not a created being as some heresies claim. He is God—Creator God. He created it all—the whole enchilada—with just a word. He said, "Let light be, and light became." Look out your window and see what He made.

His creative power sets Him apart from every other created being–every angel, every prophet. He is unique.

Have an "I know the Creator personally" day today.

5

The Son is the radiance of God's glory and the exact representation of his being, sustaining all things by his powerful word. After he had provided purification for sins, he sat down at the right hand of the Majesty in heaven.
Hebrews 1:3

Good morning friends. It's downright cold on the porch this morning, chillier than yesterday.

There is no one like Jesus. In Hebrews, chapter one, we've noticed He is the heir of all things, the creator of all things, and in verse three we discover another trait of unique Jesus: "The Son is the radiance of God's glory and the exact representation of His being."

Jesus is the radiating glory of God. Radiate means to spread or circulate. Jesus glows with God's glory. The magnificence of God is seen in the Son. But Jesus is not only a mirror of God; He is God.

The word translated "exact representation" is a term to describe the imprint of a seal or stamp. When used, a stamp leaves an exact representation of the shape, form, and size of the stamp itself. Jesus said, "If you have seen me, you have seen the Father. I and the Father are one." He is not "like" God. He "is" God.

Since Jesus dwells in us, we also display the exact image of God. Jesus's stamp is on your life, on display for all to see. Shine brightly.

Have a "radiating" day today.

6

The Son is the radiance of God's glory and the exact representation of his being, sustaining all things by his powerful word. After he had provided purification for sins, he sat down at the right hand of the Majesty in heaven.
Hebrews 1:3

Good morning. Ah, the coffee is refreshing as we sit on the porch today.

There is no one like Jesus. Remember? He is heir of all things, the Creator of everything, the brightness of God's glory, and the exact representation of God's being. The fifth unique trait of Jesus is that He sustains "all things by His powerful word."

Think about the magnitude of that statement. He sustains all things simply by His words, by His powerful voice. The translators had a dilemma when they came to the Greek word that is translated "sustains" because we don't have an English word that is as descriptive as the Greek word. The closest equivalent is "He continually causes everything to continue." He not only sustains, He moves everything along to the fulfillment of His purpose—and He only uses His Word to do it. Each tiny atom moves at His command. If He ever stops commanding, everything stops. Not a grain of sand blows, not a raindrop falls, not a snowflake floats. In the beginning, He said, "Let light be, and light became." (See Genesis 1.) Your next breath is dependent upon His command. Kind of makes you stop and say, "Wow, there really is no one like Jesus."

Have a "sustained" day today.

7

The Son is the radiance of God's glory and the exact representation of his being, sustaining all things by his powerful word. After he had provided purification for sins, he sat down at the right hand of the Majesty in heaven.
Hebrews 1:3

Good morning friends. I'm still talking about how great Jesus is. There is no one like Him. We've discovered five of the seven unique characteristics of Jesus in the first verses of the first chapter of Hebrews. He is the heir of all things, the Creator of the universe, the radiating glory of God and exact representation of God's being. He sustains and controls all things by His word. Today we discover that He "provided purification for sins."

We are not pure. We are sinners, both by nature and by our behavior. We can do nothing to purify ourselves. We are helpless to do anything about our sin stain. We cannot erase the sin we've committed. But sinless Jesus, pure and righteous, went to a cross and died there—in our place. He willingly took on the burden of our sins so we could be clothed in His righteousness. In other words, our sin was credited to His account and His purity was credited to ours. We can not cleanse ourselves, but because He was undefiled, He applied His righteousness (purity) to us. Hallelujah, what a Savior!

When I consider how Jesus took my place and made me pure, I think I might shout and end up spilling my coffee in the process.

Live a "purified" day today.

8

The Son is the radiance of God's glory and the exact representation of his being, sustaining all things by his powerful word. After he had provided purification for sins, he sat down at the right hand of the Majesty in heaven.
Hebrews 1:3

Mmm, good coffee this morning. Did I mention there is no one like Jesus?

And after giving us six phenomenal reasons why there is no one like Him, the Hebrews' writer then explains, "He sat down at the right hand of the Majesty in heaven." His place of honor in heaven, by itself, makes Him like no other.

The "right hand" of the Father refers to the position of honor, of holiness, of deity. There is only one person who sits at the right hand of the Majesty in heaven, and it's not you or me. Jesus is the only one who occupies that position.

In the Old Testament times, the high priest entered the Holy of Holies to offer sacrifice for the forgiveness of sins. The entire time he was in there, he stood. Hebrews 10:11 explains that the priests stood in the temple "daily" offering sacrifices. There were no chairs or places to sit in the sanctuary to symbolize that the priest's job was never finished. The priest did the same thing—offered the same sacrifices—day after day. He did not sit down, because he was continually offering sacrifices.

But when Jesus finished the sacrifice that paid for the sins of the world, He sat down. One of the last words spoken by Jesus on the cross was the single word in the Greek language, "Tetelestai." The word is interpreted "it is finished." (See John 19:30.) Since Jesus' death on the cross was a one-time sacrifice, once for all, there was no need for continuing sacrifice. Therefore, He took His seat at the Father's side. Everything that needed to be done for man's redemption was done. There is no need for any other sacrifice. He paid the entire debt. It is finished.

And we are seated with Him. "And God raised us up with Christ and seated us with him in the heavenly realms in Christ Jesus" (Ephesians 2:6). We are identified with Him as His child and there is no more work that can be done to make us anymore His child than we are when we accept His death for us. Therefore, we take our place of rest with Him, seated, as it were with Him.

Have a "seated" day today.

9

We must pay the most careful attention, therefore, to what we have heard, so that we do not drift away.
Hebrews 2:1

Do you remember saying something like this to one of your kids, "Now pay attention, I'm teaching you something"? I smile when I hear a mom say to her children, "Look at me. Look at me." Parents mold the character and values of children, but children must listen and respond.

So, here's a thought. How close do you pay attention when your Father speaks? Do you look at Him and listen?

It's so easy to get busy with day-to-day activities and relationships. So busy that we don't pay attention to Him. So busy that we drift away. Busyness isn't our only enemy because sometimes we waste hours on the computer or TV or some other trivial pursuit. Drifting is an unstable way to live. No anchor, no direction, no destination. But when we pay careful attention to what we have heard, we can stay anchored. To pay attention means to consider and reflect on God's Word. When you read God's Word, do you really pay attention to what you read and think about it? Someone has likened the process of reflecting on God's Word to the process of digestion in a cow's four chambered stomach. The cow eats the grass, then lays down. As the food works it's way through the chambers, the cow brings it back up and "chews the cud." That may be a disgusting analogy, but it is pretty accurate. You "ruminate" on the Word. You take it in by reading, meditating, hearing, or memorizing it, and then you think about it, bringing it back to your mind, and contemplating it's practical meaning in your life. Then you "do the Word." All of these connections with the Word are ways to pay attention to His Word.

To pay attention means to not only talk to God but also to listen to His replies. You can see God in the wonder of answered prayer and beauty of creation. Instead of drifting, see the colors and beauty around you, read His Word, pray, listen, and feel the touch of His Holy Spirit.

Have an "attentive" day today.

10

For since the message spoken through angels was binding, and every violation and disobedience received its just punishment, how shall we escape if we ignore so great a salvation?
Hebrews 2:2-3

Top o' the morning to you. I hope your day is off to a good start.

Have you ever run across a question that stumped you? A question with no easy answer? Hebrews poses that kind of question to us this morning.

"How shall we escape if we ignore so great a salvation?" The ultimate penalty of sin traps us. We deserve the punishment—the death penalty—but Christ provides escape. Through Him, we avoid the second death, which is eternal separation from God. Don't ignore His offer of escape; believe the message of Hebrews.

It's like being one of two people in an airplane. There is only one parachute aboard. The plane is going down and will crash. The pilot insists that you take his parachute and jump. You have a decision to make. The pilot has made a way of escape for you. If you stay, it is certain death. If you jump with the only parachute, you escape. The pilot is giving you a way of escape by being willing to die, even though it is his parachute. The only question is will you take the way of escape? If you choose not to take it, you can't blame the pilot.

Salvation is yours because the punishment you deserved was taken by Christ. You and I can escape because he provided the way.

Have an "escaped" day today.

11

Both the one who makes people holy and those who are made holy are of the same family. So Jesus is not ashamed to call them brothers and sisters.
Hebrews 2:11

I had a tough night last night. I was trying to watch the World Series, but it seems that I kept falling asleep. I would get comfortable with my team in the lead and drift off. And every time I did, the other team would score and tie the game. The cheers of the opposing fans would bring me back. I'd wake up and worry about my team again.

The World Series brings out the family in all of us. The Cardinal family roots for St. Louis and the Ranger family pulls for Texas. Each family identifies with their team. Two guys might be at odds with each other over something unrelated to baseball, yet they will pull together for their family team.

How does family work out in Christianity? Hebrews explains how Jesus feels about family, "so Jesus is not ashamed to call them [us] brothers and sisters." I am so glad we are in His family. We become one with the One who made us holy. He is not ashamed to identify us and identify with us. What about you? You're not ashamed to jump up and yell, "Go Rangers, I'm a Ranger fan!" or "Go Cards, I'm a Cards fan!"

Are you quick to identify yourself as part of His family? Jesus is not ashamed to say, "Dick? Yeah, he's part of my family." I should do the same for Him. Oneness or unity does not mean uniformity. It means we have a common identity that brings us together. Our fellowship, our unity, our oneness is in a common relationship with Jesus Christ.

Have a "family" day today.

And, oh yeah, Go Rangers.

12

> *But encourage one another daily, as long as it is called "Today," so that none of you may be hardened by sin's deceitfulness.*
> Hebrews 3:13

Good morning, good friend. Hope your coffee is as good as mine is this morning. The day stretches out before us. We don't know all that will happen. One thing we should know is that today we will have an opportunity to encourage someone.

You may not know who, or how, or what the circumstances will be, but you will have an opportunity. Will you take it? Observe and watch as you go about your day to look for someone who could use an uplifting word. "But encourage one another daily, as long as it is called 'Today.'" Every day is an opportunity to make someone's day. How will you do it? A word? A hug? A friendly smile? A phone call or an email? Your encouragement might be the key to another person's success today.

There is an additional benefit not only to others but to ourselves, "so that none of you may be hardened by sin's deceitfulness." Choosing to encourage others can overcome our tendency to get hardened and insensitive by the sin and circumstances around us.

Reach out to those you meet today. Your encouragement might be the little stirring that will keep them—and you—from getting crusty.

I hate when the crust on my bread becomes "crusty." A little hardness may be good for protection, but when the bread sits in the breadbox or the package and is not used for a long time, the hardness sets in and makes it tough to eat.

Sitting in your "package" and preventing your words and actions from encouraging others, makes you a little too hard. When you see discouragement in others and fail to encourage them, both you and they will become hard. Be a blessing to someone else today and you'll be more appetizing in the process.

Have an "encouraging" day today.

13

*So we see that they were not able to enter
(into His rest), because of their unbelief.*
Hebrews 3:19

Good morning. I heard about a man who constantly complained in his public prayers because he was tired and unappreciated. One day, the pastor said, "Someday we are going to bury you out here in the cemetery and you can just rest and rest and rest."

The man stood up slowly and in his most tired, complaining voice said, "Yeah, pastor, but as sure as you did, in the morning would be resurrection day."

Our Hebrews verse today describes how we can enter into God's rest. When God says we can rest in Him, these are not empty words. The word rest usually means that a person has ceased from some kind of wearisome work or worry.

To enter into His rest or to rest in Him means we can let go of our self-sufficiency and relax, because we know that He is walking with us, providing for us, living in us, and loving through us. We don't have to strive or work, in order to get His approval or acceptance. We already have it. It is living in a position of rest, resting in and on Him.

Some of us are restless because of our fears, our striving, and our insecurities. We allow the fear of man, the fear of failure, the fear of being left alone, or a thousand other fears to rule our lives.

Fear is a hard taskmaster. It never lets us relax and rest. Fear is often the result of unbelief. A failure to trust Christ for salvation will result in missing the eternal rest, and a failure to believe Him daily will result in missing practical rest.

Resting from our fears and insecurities helps us spiritually and emotionally in the same way that ceasing from physical work helps us physically. Letting go of fear allows us to recover spiritually and emotionally and trains us to depend on God's promises rather than our emotions. Rest helps us to release the negative emotions piled one upon another in our lives. Do you remember, as a child, how comforting and reassuring it was to climb up onto your mom's or dad's lap, put your arms around him or her and feel the strength and security? Somehow you knew Mom or Dad would take care of everything.

Jesus has provided a way for you to climb up into your heavenly Father's lap and rest. Let go and trust Him.

Have a "restful" day today.

14

For the word of God is alive and active. Sharper than any double-edged sword, it penetrates even to dividing soul and spirit, joints and marrow; it judges the thoughts and attitudes of the heart.
Hebrews 4:12

Did you read in the Word this morning? Each day, God has an exciting message for you. It may be a word of encouragement, a piece of guidance, a rebuke, an expression of comfort, or an instruction. He has a fresh, living word every minute of every day.

John called Jesus the Word. "In the beginning was the Word, and the Word was with God and the Word was God" (John 1:1). Putting this verse from John together with our Hebrews verse for today (4:12) means Jesus Himself is alive and active in your life today, because He is the Word and His Word is alive and active today. Imagine the possibilities. He is alive and He lives in you. What could you do today with the vitality and wisdom of Jesus?

Don't live like a dead person or a person without hope. Refuse sadness, depression, or lifelessness. Instead let Jesus stir up your creative juices. Dream big dreams.

Live each day full of joy and compassion and activity. Be alive and active because His Word is in you.

Have an "alive" day today.

15

> *For the word of God is alive and active. Sharper than any double-edged sword, it penetrates even to dividing soul and spirit, joints and marrow; it judges the thoughts and attitudes of the heart.*
> Hebrews 4:12

The coffee is nice and hot.

Someone suggested I might be a little judgmental. Me? Judgmental? Imagine that. I thought I was just "telling it like it was." But the truth is sometimes I tell it like I think it should be. The indictment is right. When it comes to the actions of another, I can judge what those actions say to me, but I can't see into the heart of the person. I don't know his or her real motivation or the condition of his or her heart. Only God can see like that. And He sees into us through His Word, "it [The Word] judges the thoughts and attitudes of the heart" (Hebrews 4:12). His Word cuts through all the posturing and pretense to see the real heart.

So maybe I was judging, and then again, maybe the person who judged me to be judgmental was judging me. Do you notice some circular judging going on here? Maybe the safest thing is to encourage each other to get into the Word and let the Word judge us all.

Have a "judged" day today.

16

*Nothing in all creation is hidden from God's sight.
Everything is uncovered and laid bare before the
eyes of him to whom we must give account.*
Hebrews 4:13

Good morning, friends. We had our first freeze in the Hill Country this morning. Hope you are well and warm. I am enjoying the fire and a cup of hot coffee.

As I read in Hebrews this morning, I thought about our reluctance to confess before God. The word "confess" actually means "to say along with" or "to agree with."

Yet we think our confession is letting God in on a secret He didn't already know. "God, you will never believe what I did Thursday night, but I…."

He was there. He saw it all. There is nothing you can hide from Him. So go ahead and agree with Him about it. "Nothing in all creation is hidden from God's sight" (Hebrews 4:13). What a frightening thought! Everything is unhidden. He sees all. Actually, the idea of God seeing all should not be scary. It is the best thing because He will see when we are starting down the wrong path and direct us to the right way.

Admitting your sin helps you. Confession is not prescribed for God's benefit but for ours. Pardon is available through Christ's death on the cross.

So give an account and have an "unhidden" day today.

17

*Therefore, since we have a great high priest who
has ascended into heaven, Jesus the Son of
God, let us hold firmly to the faith we profess.*
Hebrews 4:14

Good morning from the front porch of The Creek House. I'm sipping my coffee, watching the wildlife, and praising the Lord for His goodness. Sometimes the counsel we get from Christian advice-givers can be confusing. When we are going through a difficulty, one person will tell us to "just hold on," while another person tells us, "just let go." Well which is it? Do we hold on or do we let go?

And the answer is, "Yes."

We hold on to our faith in Jesus Christ; "let us hold firmly to the faith we profess" (Hebrews 4:14). Holding firmly to our faith means we look for the promises of God in Scripture. Once we find the promise that applies to our lives or situation, we believe it, rest upon it, and if necessary, act on it. When we believe in, act upon, or wait for a promise from God's Word, we are holding on to the faith we profess. Our faith is based on the reality that Jesus Christ, the Son of God, died on the cross, was buried, and rose again, in order that we might have forgiveness of sins, eternal life, and a restored relationship with God. When we believe, we become His child and trust Him to supply all our needs. Hold on to that.

What do we let go of? Dependence on ourselves. When you take hold of Christ by faith, you relinquish control; then you find He is already holding on to you. He will never let you go. You can release all your self-sufficiency to His sufficiency. He's got you, so hold on and let go.

Look, Ma, no hands!

Have a "holding on, letting go" day today.

18

For we do not have a high priest who is unable to empathize with our weaknesses, but we have one who has been tempted in every way, just as we are—yet he did not sin.
Hebrews 4:15

Good morning. Has anyone ever said something like this to you when you were trying to encourage him or her? "Well, you just don't understand what I'm going through."

We don't always know what the other person's life is like. We haven't experienced his pain or her loss. We don't truly know the depth of his hurt or disappointment or her rejection. We haven't lived in his or her shoes and experienced the same difficulty or emotions.

Someone knows exactly what it's like to be in your position. Hebrews explains, "For we do not have a high priest who is unable to empathize with our weaknesses, but we have one who has been tempted in every way, just as we are—yet he did not sin" (Hebrews 4:15). He has experienced every temptation you face—victoriously.

Now He is here to walk you through your tough time. He knows. He understands. He has answers to your difficulties and gives grace to handle your pain.

He may even send someone with skin on to encourage you.

Have a "someone understands" day today.

19

*Let us then approach God's throne of grace with
confidence, so that we may receive mercy and find
grace to help us in our time of need.*
Hebrews 4:16

Good morning from the beautiful Hill Country of Texas. Hope your day is off to a good start. But what if it isn't off to a good start or what if today holds unknown struggles, heartaches, and needs?

Well be encouraged, my friend, because there's an app for that. Actually there really is an application you can take advantage of during your time of need, and you don't buy it at the iTunes store. You simply lift your voice to your Father in the name of your Savior, Jesus Christ.

Really? Just call on Him?

Yes, the verse is clear. Call on Him in confidence. Step right up and voice your concerns. He has given you an invitation. Not only has He invited you, He has also opened the path to Him through prayer. He is listening and He cares.

We have access and an invitation. "Let us then approach God's throne of grace with confidence, so that we may receive mercy and find grace to help us in our time of need" (Hebrews 4:16).

Chances are you are going to need mercy and grace today. Go get it. He encourages us to approach the throne.

Have a "confident" day today.

20

*During the days of Jesus' life on earth, he offered
up prayers and petitions with fervent cries and tears
to the one who could save him from death, and he
was heard because of his reverent submission. Son
though he was, he learned obedience from what he suffered.*
Hebrews 5:7-8

Good morning. Have you ever wondered if there was any purpose in the pain and discomfort of life? Sometimes we feel no one else has ever experienced the same hurt, pain, or disappointment we have faced. But Jesus understands.

How could that be? He was God. Surely He had no problems.

He was also a man. He was all God and all man. As man, He lived through all the same kinds of experiences as you and I. Remember the Garden of Gethsemane? Jesus experienced first-hand what it meant to cry out in the midst of suffering. Throughout His life He dealt with pain, grief, and sorrow by calling out to His Father. "During the days of Jesus' life on earth, he offered up prayers and petitions with fervent cries and tears to the one who could save him from death, and he was heard because of his reverent submission. Son though he was, he learned obedience from what he suffered" (Hebrews 5:7-8 NIV).

Did I read that right? Jesus, though God's son, learned obedience by suffering? What about you? Have you learned obedience as a result of your tough times? Obedience is God's goal for your life. When we obey, He is pleased. John recorded what Jesus taught about obedience, "Anyone who loves me will obey my teaching. My Father will love them, and we will come to them and make our home with them" (John 14:23).

Have a "learning" day today.

21

*In fact, though by this time you ought to be teachers,
you need someone to teach you the elementary truths
of God's word all over again. You need milk, not solid food!*
Hebrews 5:12

Hope your coffee is good this morning. Let me ask you a question: Got milk? The question drives every English teacher crazy. Good grammarians want to correct the grammar to, "Do you have any milk?" Trust me, I'm going somewhere with this. Stay with me. Look what the Hebrews' writer had to say about milk.

"In fact, though by this time you ought to be teachers, you need someone to teach you the elementary truths of God's word all over again. You need milk, not solid food!" (Hebrews 5: 12).

Raising children isn't easy, but parents understand that a child shouldn't stay on the milk bottle forever. At a certain point, we start feeding our children a more substantial diet.

I read about a guy who, as an adult, insisted on wearing a diaper and eating baby food. I thought the report was tragic; then I considered how many professing Christians are spiritually in the same shape. We may have grown old in the Christian faith but still behave and understand like babies. Growing up spiritually means maturing into devoted, faithful, dedicated adults.

Maturing in Christ doesn't happen accidentally. It is something we purpose to do. You have to want to grow. I know, I've been there. If you don't want to mature, you won't. It's really that simple. But if you are still drinking the milk of Christianity, the Word says, "Earnestly desire the sincere milk of the word that you may grow thereby." So this morning, right now, when it comes to wanting to grow more in Christ, got milk?

Have a "meaty" day today.

22

Therefore let us move beyond the elementary teachings about Christ and be taken forward to maturity.
Hebrews 6:1

The weather is freezing in the Texas Hill Country this morning, so I'm not outside on the porch. Instead, I am feeling toasty by the fire.

I remember being a little confused when I was a teenager. My mom often hugged me and called me her baby. (I was the youngest of three boys.) Then my dad would come into the room and say, "Act your age." If that wasn't puzzling enough, then one of my brothers would say, "Why don't you grow up?" Confusing.

Living spiritually can be confusing too. Sometimes we want to be a baby and snuggle up in the arms of the Lord. And sometimes we want or need to be mature. Other times we hunger to develop way beyond our years. According to today's verse, we should desire to "move beyond the elementary teachings about Christ and be taken forward to maturity."

The key word is desire. I think as long as we desire to mature, we are on the right track. Like the theme song of the old George Jefferson sitcom, "Moving on Up," as long as we are moving on while we are moving up, we'll be where He wants us to be.

Maturity takes more than knowledge and information alone. We also have to experience life, whether easy or tough. Sometimes the experiences are a little uncomfortable, but maturing is marked by encounters.

So go ahead and have a "moving to maturity" day today.

23

It is impossible for those who have once been enlightened, who have tasted the heavenly gift, who have shared in the Holy Spirit, who have tasted the goodness of the word of God and the powers of the coming age and who have fallen away, to be brought back to repentance.
Hebrews 6:4-6

Hope you're having a good week. The writer of Hebrews poses a big question in our verse today. What about the security of the believer? Is it possible to be saved by grace and then be lost again by works? The writer reveals that the answer is, "No." In fact, getting unsaved is an impossibility. Salvation is eternal because it is totally dependent upon what Christ has done for us, not what we do or don't do for Him. The writer of Hebrews sets it up as an "if – then" proposition. "If" it were possible to be lost after being saved, "then" it would be impossible to be saved again, because Jesus would need to be crucified again.

We in the evangelical community say, "Once saved, always saved."

Do you see the impossibility? What good would the sacrifice of Christ on the cross, be if it could be negated by my falling away? So live in confidence in the sacrifice of Jesus and trust Him to keep you no matter what happens.

Have a "saved" day today.

24

God did this so that, by two unchangeable things in which it is impossible for God to lie, we who have fled to take hold of the hope set before us may be greatly encouraged. We have this hope as an anchor for the soul, firm and secure.
Hebrews 6:18-19

Good morning. I hope you're not running as late as I am today. But coffee is good anytime of the day.

Did you hear about the two antelope grazing on the range (you know, where the deer and the antelope play)? One happened to overhear the hunter say to his friend, "I think I can hit him from here."

The one antelope said to the other, "I think I just heard a discouraging word."

Like coffee, encouragement is also good any time of the day. In our verse today, the writer of Hebrews gives great encouragement concerning the promise of our salvation. The only way I can lose what God has given me in salvation would be if He were lying to me. Guess what? It is impossible for God to lie. So I can be assured that when He says my salvation is eternal and it is by His grace, then it is.

This hope ought to be an anchor in your life. Where is your soul anchored? In your own abilities, or passion, or compassion, or works? That's a flimsy anchor, my friend. We have an Anchor, firm and secure.

That is an encouraging word if I ever heard one.

Have an "anchored" day today.

25

The former regulation is set aside because it was weak and useless (for the law made nothing perfect), and a better hope is introduced, by which we draw near to God.
Hebrews 7:18, 19

Sometimes we sacrifice the best on the altar of the good. We involve ourselves in activities or habits that are not bad, but the time and effort spent on these good things may keep us from involving ourselves in the best. For example, we can spend our Sunday mornings watching a worship service on television, which is good, or we can attend a worship service with other believers, which is better. Here's another example. We can give our volunteer time working through a totally secular service club, which is good, or we can use that same time serving with the church, which is better. Or a final example: we can spend all of our reading time with an interesting book, which is good, or we can spend some of that time in the Word of God, which is better.

Sometimes we also try to impress God by doing good things but doing them for the wrong reasons. Sometimes we put on our best behavior because we think we will please or amaze God.

Nothing we do impresses God, and you will wear yourself out trying to do good when God has something better in mind. When we understand that our salvation is based on what He has done for us rather than what we do for him, our view of God and His gift to us changes; and according to today's verse, we draw nearer to God. Later in verse 22, we receive a guarantee, "Because of this oath, Jesus has become the guarantor of a better covenant." He has replaced the system of law (works), which is good in and of itself, with a better hope. He has guaranteed a better covenant for you. Don't settle for good.

Have a "better" day today.

26

Therefore he is able to save completely those who come to God through him, because he always lives to intercede for them.
Hebrews 7:25

Morning from the Hill Country of Texas.

What's left on your bucket list? Do you intend to climb a mountain or dive to the depths of the ocean? Maybe your list includes visiting all the professional baseball parks in the country or learning to play guitar or piano. All of us have lists, and most of us haven't completed those lists yet. I start projects that somehow don't get finished. Oh, I will finish them. I just don't know when.

Jesus left nothing unfinished. He is able and saves "completely." Another verse reminds us "He who has begun a good thing in us will bring it to completion."

I went to a seminar many years ago where the leader used the letters, PBPWMGINFY. The letters stand for "Please Be Patient with Me, God Is Not Finished Yet." While the statement is true about how He builds new depth and wisdom into our lives daily, He has nothing more to do when it comes to our salvation. He has completed the job.

He's working on everything about you, except your salvation. Your redemption and your eternity are a done deal.

Have a "completed" day today.

27

*Let us hold unswervingly to the hope we profess,
for he who promised is faithful.*
Hebrews 10:23

I hope everyone is off to a good day. I'm running a little bit late this morning, but it's never too late for a daily visit. The writer of Hebrews encouraged us to "hold unswervingly to the hope we profess."

There is nothing we can count on without question in this world, but there is something in the coming world we can absolutely count on. Read the end of today's verse again, "He who promised is faithful." So let us hold onto Him. He is our hope. We must never let go even when distractions seem more real and present.

The difference between wishing and hoping is basis. Have you ever wished for something, but had no basis for its fulfillment? I am a football fan. If I were to say, "I wish my team would win the national championship after they have lost three games," I would be wishing without basis. If I were to say, "I hope my team wins the next game," I have a hope based on a distinct possibility.

Hope also has as its basis the object toward which

hope is projected. In this case, our hope is directed toward God. Hope is not a wish but a confident expectation that what God has already said is true.

Let us have a "hope without question" day today.

28

And let us consider how we may spur one another on toward love and good deeds, not giving up meeting together, as some are in the habit of doing, but encouraging one another—and all the more as you see the Day approaching.
Hebrews 10:24, 25

Good morning, all.

As we continue to look at the "let us" commands in Hebrews 10, we find a challenge. First the writer told us to draw near to God, and hold to our faith. Now he challenges us to give encouragement to others.

So give thought (consider) how you can reassure or praise another person. Then do it intentionally (spur one another). Cover your encouraging words and deeds in love.

To "spur someone" means to urge and support him or her, not to irritate. Our words can build up or tear down. When we encourage another person, we give hope. So don't wait. Do it today, with urgency, living in the light of His soon return. Find someone to challenge and encourage today.

Have a "spurring on" day today.

To me, the smell of fresh-made coffee is one of the greatest inventions.

—Hugh Jackman

29

It is a dreadful thing to fall into the hands of the living God.
Hebrews 10: 31

Good morning. What's your worst nightmare? I mean aside from Alabama and LSU playing one more football game this season. What are you most afraid of? Even the toughest guys have some fears even though they may never talk about it.

If you are really a child of God, let me take away one big fear. It's a good news – bad news deal. The good news is that as His child, you don't have to fear being in God's presence or under His authority. The bad news is: if you don't know Him, you ought to be shaking in your boots.

God is solemn about sin; He takes it seriously. Everyone who scoffs at God, who laughs at the idea of faith, who follows other gods, or who expects to enter Heaven any other way except through Jesus Christ will discover a whole new meaning to the word "dreadful." I'd rather be in the arms of a loving God as His child than in the hands of the living, holy God as one who has rejected him. Because of His love, we don't have to dread.

Have an "unfearful" day today.

Coffee and Friends: A Perfect Blend

30

So do not throw away your confidence; it will be richly rewarded.
Hebrews 10:35

When is the last time you went through a closet or a drawer or a box and threw a bunch of stuff away because you didn't use it anymore? We usually throw away or give away stuff we don't need. We even call these items "cast offs."

There is one thing we shouldn't cast off: confidence in God's promises. Did you know that there is a promise in God's Word that, in some way, speaks to every need you have?

Do you need wisdom. He has a promise for that. "If any of you lack wisdom, let him ask of God, that giveth to all men liberally, and upbraideth not; and it shall be given him" (James 1:5).

Do you need some provision? "But my God shall supply all your need according to his riches in glory by Christ Jesus" (Philippians 4:19).

And these are just two examples. The Word of God is filled with His promises. The issue is not the promises of God, but your confidence in those promises. Confidence is faith—complete trust in God even if circumstances are hard. If you have a need, God has a supply. He delights in meeting your every need. If you haven't used your faith in a while, don't throw it away. It's the only thing in your life that is just as good now as the day you acquired it.

So don't throw it away, hang on to it.

Have a "holding on" day today.

31

*Now faith is confidence in what we hope for and
assurance about what we do not see.*
Hebrews 11:1

Good morning, everyone. Hope your coffee tastes as good as mine does on this crisp windy morning in the Hill Country.

What is your definition of faith? Have you ever wished for more faith or greater faith? I have. According to Scripture, each one of us has a "measure" of faith. (See Romans 12:3.) And that small amount of faith will remove mountains—not because of the size of that faith but because of the object of our faith, Jesus Christ.

I like the writer of Hebrews' definition of faith. Faith is confidence. The definition of confidence is sure, certain, and buoyant. The basis of our hope, as believers, is not wishful thinking. Rather, the basis of our hope is in God Himself. If He has said something in Scripture that is ours to claim, then it is not wishful thinking, but a certainty that it will come.

Even though we may not be able to "see" it or "experience" it immediately. Remember, our timetable is not always God's timetable. As someone has observed, "God may be late, but He's always on time, His time." We don't see our home in heaven yet, but we know, based on His Word, that it is there, reserved for us. Our bodies are wearing out, but we know that He has said we will have a new body. We don't "see" it yet, but our "hope" is settled.

And Romans chapter eight reminds us that if we can see something, we are really not exercising faith. To paraphrase my friend Manley Beasley, "faith is believing that something is so, when it is not so, in order for it to be so, because with God, it is so."

So, figure out what "is so" with God and then put your confidence in that.

Have a "certainty" day today.

32

*By faith we understand that the universe was
formed at God's command, so that what is seen
was not made out of what was visible.*
Hebrews 11:3

Good morning, good friends. I don't know about you but, sometimes I grow weary of the arguments from science that, if something is believed "by faith," it is somehow not intellectual. We live by faith every day. You get on an airplane; you have faith it will fly. An intellectual says, "But the law of aerodynamics is scientific." Maybe so, but there's a pilot up there that you have never met and have no idea of his condition or skill. So you trust him, by faith.

Then you go to a doctor, whose name you can't pronounce, get a piece of paper with something written on it that you can't read, take it to a little window, give it to a pharmacist you've never met, receive medicine in a bottle that if taken in the wrong amount, can kill you. Then you take it home and swallow it.

These examples are faith at work.

Empirical science requires a fact to be repeatable and observable. Creation is neither. Faith accepts that God did it in His way. Or you believe that by random chance gases came together creating a big bang, and poof, the world was born. The latter takes more faith than the former.

One of the major arguments for the existence of God is called the "argument from design" or "the teleological argument." This concept simply states that an ordered universe demands an ordered mind behind it. That is, if left to chance, a weaker or stronger "big bang" and the universe would not have turned out as it did and would not be inhabitable for humans. But because the universe is ordered and it is designed in a way that man inhabits it, one might say that it was "made for us." One mile closer to the sun and we would burn up, and mile further away and we would freeze. A one or two degree in the change of the earth's axis and nothing is the same. Now if you are stumbling a little over this, just look at a new born baby and realize that God really did know us from our mother's womb.

Have another "creation" day today.

33

> *By faith Abel brought God a better offering than Cain did. By faith he was commended as righteous, when God spoke well of his offerings. And by faith Abel still speaks, even though he is dead.*
> Hebrews 11:4

Good morning, would you like another cup of coffee? Well get up and go get it. Just kidding.

"I'm doing the best I can." Have you ever heard or said those words? Some folks say something similar when referring to going to heaven. "Well, God will let me into heaven because He's a loving God and I'm doing the best I can."

It has never occurred to these well-meaning people that the very best they can do is not good enough. In Genesis 4:1-5, when Cain and Abel came to bring an offering to God, each brought something that was the result of their vocation. Cain tilled the soil while Abel raised sheep. Abel brought the fruit of his own sweat and toil. His offering was rejected. Abel, on the other hand brought an offering that represented a life sacrificed.

What made Abel's offering better than Cain's? From his own farming effort, Cain brought the very best he could do. Abel brought an innocent animal to which God had given life. It was the best God could do.

God doesn't ask us to bring the best we can do. He asks us to surrender to Him so that He can do His work in and through us. His demand is the best He can do through us, not the best that we can do for Him.

Have an "Abel" kind of day today.

34

By faith Enoch was taken from this life, so that he did not experience death; he could not be found, because God had taken him away. For before he was taken, he was commended as one who pleased God. And without faith it is impossible to please God, because anyone who comes to him must believe that he exists and that he rewards those who earnestly seek him.
Hebrews 11:5-6

The entire eleventh chapter of Hebrews centers on the subject of faith. In these verses, Enoch is commended as "one who pleased God."

Do you realize that the highest goal of man is not to be happy? Now I know that this may come as a shock, but God is more interested in our holiness than He is in our happiness. There is a difference between positional righteousness and practical holiness. Positional righteousness is what has been deposited in our account, because of Christ's death on the cross. Practical holiness is what happens when we allow Christ to live through us. Practical holiness means our actions, our words, our thoughts, are what He wants us to to do, to say, or to think. In order for us to reach practical holiness, God may have to knock off the things in our life that do not look like Christ. And He sometimes uses tough times, uneasy circumstances, or unpleasant people to accomplish it in us. Therefore, our goal is not to be comfortable but to be like Him. If you live and die with happiness as your goal, it may never be said of you that "he or she was commended as one who pleased God." My goal is to please God. Someone may ask, "How in the world can you do that?"

Notice I didn't say "impress" God, or "surprise" God. I said, "please Him." How? By faith. By exercising even the tiniest portion of faith. I simply live my life in the confident assurance that God exists, I am His, and it's worth my time to seek Him. And that pleases God.

Have a "pleasing" day today.

35

By faith Noah, when warned about things not yet seen, in holy fear built an ark to save his family. By his faith he condemned the world and became heir of the righteousness that is in keeping with faith.
Hebrews 11:7

Some friends brought us some southern pecan coffee beans. Fresh ground. Nothing like the aroma. Love the taste. What flavor are you drinking this morning?

There is a scene in the old movie, *Hondo* where John Wayne warns a little boy about his cur dog and tells the little guy that the dog doesn't like being petted and will bite him. After several warnings, the little boy touched the dog and the dog bit him.

The mother said, "Why did you let him touch the dog? You knew he would be bitten."

To which John Wayne replied, "He won't touch him again."

How many warnings has our Lord given us about the consequences of sin? Noah's faith in God allowed him to see the unseen and act accordingly. No rain had ever fallen on the earth yet Noah believed and pulled out his tool belt.

God warns us too. Will you listen and follow His instructions? Believing the unseen is a faith operation. As a matter of fact, all of life is a faith operation.

Have a "seeing the unseen" day today.

36

By faith Abraham, when called to go to a place…obeyed and went, even though he did not know where he was going.
Hebrews 11:8

Hope you are off to a good start this morning. Hebrews 11 is known as the "faith" chapter and for good reason. The faith life is walking, not by sight, but by trust. Most of us want God's will for our lives. So we pray, "Lord, show me your will." That's noble, but what we sometimes mean is, "Lord, show me your will, so that I can decide if I want to follow it."

Abraham gave us a great example of following God. Some might call Abraham a man of blind faith. I believe he kept his eyes on God rather than on his circumstances. Notice the sequence: called, obeyed, went. Then he got to where he was supposed to be.

Do you look at God rather than your situation? Do you move forward with your plans or move toward God's call? Go on, obey His calling. You can trust Him.

Have an "trusting" day today.

I sleep just to wake up for coffee!

—Unknown

37

> *All these people were still living by*
> *faith when they died.*
> Hebrews 11:13

Those fresh ground southern pecan coffee beans sure know how to say good morning to me.

In the eleventh chapter of Hebrews, we have been looking at the subject of faith. Don't rush past verse thirteen. I'm not sure, but I think I might want those words on my headstone when I'm buried. I was going to go with "I kept telling y'all I was sick," but I like this better.

Some say that the most important thing is how you live. Others say that the most important thing is how you die. A country song combines the two, "Live Like You Were Dying."

I like the idea, because we all are. Dying, I mean. We don't sit around drinkin' RC colas and eatin' moon pies and talkin' about who's going to die next, but we are all in the process of dying.

My greatest desire is to finish my life well. To my dying day, I want people to see Christ in my life. To hear His hope in my words. To feel His love in my actions. To be drawn to His Word in my teaching. I want my children and grandchildren to say that my life influenced them to walk closer to Christ. I want to live in such a way that when God is ready for me and my earth suit quits working, folks will say, "He was still living by faith when he died." How about you?

Have a "living and dying by faith" day today.

38

Instead, they were longing for a better country—a heavenly one. Therefore God is not ashamed to be called their God, for he has prepared a city for them.
Hebrews 13:16

Where is your focus today? Is it on the next minute, the next hour, or the next day? Or is it on the next life—the heavenly one?

We preachers tell our listeners not to be ashamed of Christ. We love to quote Romans 1:16, "For I am not ashamed of the gospel, for it is the power of God unto salvation." And our preaching is true, but we also need to remember it is a two-way street.

Please don't misunderstand my thought here. While we are on this earth, living this life, we want to live in such a way as to please God. That means allowing Him to live His life through us. I am so glad that God is not ashamed to be called my God, because of who I am in Christ. But I also want to live in such a way, that there would never be a question of shame. We talk a lot about being ashamed to speak out or to identify ourselves as a Christian. The question is not so much whether I am ashamed of God or of being a Christian, but whether there would ever be a reason for God to be ashamed of me.

He is not ashamed of you. You are His child. Therefore, keep your eyes on the finish line, "looking unto Jesus, the author and finisher of our faith," and long for a better country, a heavenly one and make God proud of you.

Have a "longing" day today.

39

He who had embraced the promises was about to sacrifice his one and only son, even though God had said to him, 'It is through Isaac that your offspring will be reckoned.
Hebrews 11:17-18

I admit there are some things in Scripture that perplex me. One of them is God's command to Abraham that he sacrifice Isaac. I can't fathom this directive for the man of God to kill his son.

It is also hard to understand why God gave His one and only Son for me.

I'm not sure that I would have passed the test like Abraham did. What I hope to learn by reading Abraham's story is simple obedience by faith.

I love to play the guitar. I have always owned rather inexpensive guitars. One day I was in a music store admiring the Taylor guitars, very expensive instruments. As I walked out, I said in my heart, "Thank you Lord, for the instrument I have. Yet, you can provide one of those for me when you desire." That week, a man walked up the path to the church carrying a guitar case. He put it down at my feet and said, "I don't know why, but the Lord put it on my heart to give you my guitar." I opened the case to see a perfect Taylor guitar staring back at me. That man didn't know of my prayer or thoughts, but God did. And when God laid it on his heart, he was obedient, even though he might not have understood the why of it. Here's my point: We tend to get hung up on the big points of obedience and say we don't understand it, when the truth is we are not even willing to be obedient in the simpler things of the Word. Here's a suggestion. Until God asks us to sacrifice our only son, let's "embrace the promises" and obey the simpler things that we do understand.

Have an "obedient" day today.

40

By faith Moses' parents hid him for three months after he was born, because they saw he was no ordinary child, and they were not afraid of the king's edict.
Hebrews 11:23

One of the ways we leave a blessing to our children is to encourage them to be worshippers of God on their own. If they are only living from the power of their parents' commitment to the Lord, they will never develop their own relationship of dependence upon Him.

Every Christian parent wants their children to live so as to please the Lord. We must remind them constantly that they are individuals before the Lord and uniquely loved by Him.

Moses' parents gave him to the Lord and made the hall of faith heroes in Hebrews. But look at what prompted them. "They saw he was no ordinary child." No child is ordinary, and each one needs to know we recognize how unique he or she is.

In the movie *The Help*, Abeline looked into the eyes of the child she cared for and said, "You is kind, you is smart, and you is important."

We need to tell our kids and grandkids they are God's kids. Each one is valuable and important and not ordinary.

Help your children to have a "more than an ordinary" day and life.

41

By faith Moses, when he had grown up, refused to be known as the son of Pharaoh's daughter. He chose to be mistreated along with the people of God rather than to enjoy the fleeting pleasures of sin. He regarded disgrace for the sake of Christ as of greater value than the treasures of Egypt, because he was looking ahead to his reward.
Hebrews 11:24-26

Who in their right mind, given the choice, would choose mistreatment over an exalted position? Some politicians seem willing to become anything the people want in order to be elected. It's hard to admit, but I often desire the approval of men over the approval of God. Human nature makes us want to be liked. We are consumed with what men think rather than what God knows.

Moses "regarded disgrace for the sake of Christ as of greater value than the treasures of Egypt." He could accept disgrace and even mistreatment because he looked "ahead to his reward."

Paul reminded us of this in Romans 8:18, "I consider that our present sufferings are not worth comparing with the glory that will be revealed in us." The Lord said that our treasures are not in this life, but in the next. "Do not store up for yourselves treasures on earth, where moths and vermin destroy, and where thieves break in and steal. But store up for yourselves treasures in heaven, where moths and vermin do not destroy, and where thieves do not break in and steal. For where your treasure is, there your heart will be also" (Matthew 6:19-21).

Oh Lord, help me to be wise enough not to value the treasures that don't last, but help to greatly value the treasures that never pass.

Have a "looking ahead" day today.

42

By faith the people passed through the Red Sea as on dry land; but when the Egyptians tried to do so, they were drowned. By faith the walls of Jericho fell, after the army had marched around them for seven days.
Hebrews 11:29-30

Good morning, fellow coffee drinkers. Hope your coffee is as good as mine is this morning.

Believing without seeing requires us to take a risk. We must act on our faith without always understanding why. It's a difficult concept, but it's based on an important principle about faith. Faith does not demand understanding.

When Moses finished praying and God said, "Tell the people to go forward," they did not understand what God was about to do. They didn't know God was going to roll back the waters of the Red Sea and dry it out so that they could cross on dry land and then roll it back over their pursuers. But they walked forward in faith.

Later Joshua told the people to march around Jericho once each day for six days and then to go around it seven times on the seventh day, shouting while they marched. Do you think they thought it was a good battle plan? I doubt it. But they did it anyway. Sometimes God gives us complete understanding, and sometimes He doesn't. Faith takes risks and faith obeys, even without understanding.

Have a "risky" day today.

43

By faith the prostitute Rahab, because she welcomed the spies, was not killed with those who were disobedient.
Hebrews 11:31

Good morning. I hope you are ready for a blessed day.

Have you ever asked yourself a question like, "What could God possibly do with me? How could He use me?" Our verse from Hebrews 11 today reminds us how God has a purpose for every person.

All we really need to hear are the first few words of the verse. "By faith, the prostitute Rahab." Faith qualifies you no matter your past failures.

A friend sent me a list of the Bible's failures. "Jacob was a cheater. Peter had a temper. David had an affair. Noah got drunk. Jonah ran from God. Paul was a murderer. Gideon was insecure. Miriam was a gossiper. Martha was a worrier. Thomas was a doubter. Sarah was impatient. Elijah was depressed. Moses stuttered. Zaccheus was short. Abraham was old. Lazarus was dead."

It seems there are few qualifications to receive the call of God. He doesn't call the qualified, He qualifies the called. Church is a perfect place for imperfect people.

So no matter your past failures, walk in faith today!

Have a "qualified" day today.

44

These were all commended for their faith.
Hebrews 11:39

The eleventh chapter of Hebrews has been an enlightening chapter. I especially love the way the writer closes it out. Take time to read Hebrews 11:32-38. It's as if the writer looks back over his work and sees the stories of all those who have lived the faith life and then throws up his hands, "What else can I say? There's not enough time, space, or words to describe the results of faith."

Then he tries to do it.

But listen closely to how the writer summarized all the people of faith. "These were all commended for their faith."

Not one was commended for his work. No one was commended for her results or success. The accolades didn't come for talent or ability to speak, or sing, or lead. No one was commended for his number of baptisms, or the size of the crowd he could gather, nor the size of his portfolio or the number of employees in his company. No one was commended for her knowledge. Neither was anyone condemned for past failures.

"These were all commended for their faith."

What have you done that is commendable? Absolutely nothing, unless it was rooted in and a by-product of faith.

So go have a "faith-filled" day today.

45

Therefore, since we are surrounded by such a great cloud of witnesses, let us throw off everything that hinders and the sin that so easily entangles.
Hebrews 12:1

Another Super Bowl has come and gone, and the rumor is they are going to play another one next year. How super can it be if they have to do it every year? Just kidding.

I watched it along with the biggest television crowd in history. Can you imagine the numbers of spectators? And yet the Bible teaches we are being watched by at least that many.

The image here is of a race rather than a ball game, but you get the point. Have you ever wondered why track stars don't compete in a race dressed in hockey uniforms? The bulky clothing would impede their progress, slow them down.

Same thing with the sinful habits and actions we cling to. The sins that we commit over and over, without dealing with them can become like extra heavy clothing. When we allow continual sin to "build up" in our life, it can keep us from walking in fellowship with God and keep others from seeing Jesus in us. First John 1:9 reminds us how we can be cleansed of the daily build up of sin in our lives. "If we confess our sins, he is faithful and just and will forgive us our sins and purify us from all unrighteousness." Confession is not letting God in on something of which He was unaware. It means agreeing with Him that it was sin. Then we appropriate His cleansing. We are stripped from that sin.

When Lazarus came out of the tomb at the command of Christ, the Lord said to "loose him and let him go." That meant to remove the grave clothes, those clothes that had been wrapped around him. He says the same thing to us. We are no longer living in death, but in life, so take the grave clothes (continuing sin in our lives) away. There's no need to be weighed down with continuing sin anymore.

So quit trying to run a race dressed like a hockey goalie. Lay aside, take off, throw away the sin that is weighing you down and entangling itself around you and run the race free, unimpeded.

Have a "free" day today.

46

And let us run with perseverance the race marked out for us, fixing our eyes on Jesus, the pioneer and perfecter of faith. For the joy set before him he endured the cross, scorning its shame, and sat down at the right hand of the throne of God.
Hebrews 12:1-2

Yesterday we talked about throwing off the weight of sin that so easily entangles us. Our race—the race of life—is a marathon, not a brief sprint. Our race is like an iron man triathlon. Sometimes we are running, sometimes we're swimming (or drowning), and sometimes we are riding aboard a fast vehicle. We won't finish it by the end of the day. Our race is about patience and perseverance.

There are at least three good points to take away from today's Scripture.

(1) The One who has marked out the course of our race is the Lord. And He makes no mistakes.

(2) Like a runner keeping his eyes on the finish line, we must keep our focus on the Lord Jesus, rather than on our circumstances.

(3) Our Lord has already run the ultimate race marked out for Him. He endured the cross.

The meaning of the word translated "pioneer" is a word which means "trail-blazer." You may be exhausted, but with yours eyes fixed on Jesus, you are doing well.

So have a "fixed on Him" day today.

47

For the joy set before him he endured the cross, scorning its shame, and sat down at the right hand of the throne of God. Consider him who endured such opposition from sinners, so that you will not grow weary and lose heart.
Hebrews 12:2, 3

When is the last time you felt discouraged? I mean prior to this morning? Discouragement can be a daily battle. With the demands of life, job, family, and day-to-day living, it is so easy to get discouraged.

When you are discouraged, cling to today's verse. Picture our Lord in the hours leading up to the cross, discouraged in Gethsemane, betrayed in the garden, mocked at a midnight trial, beaten and scourged most of the next day, laughed at, and ridiculed, not to mention having his beard plucked out. All of this happened before He got to the agony of Calvary, the cross, and death.

During it all, there was gladness. Why? Because He could see the joy set before Him. He could see a failed life being redeemed 2,000 years later. He could see a home and family put together. He could see past the trial and discouragement and pain to the results that would come.

One of our problems is that we can't see past our own little moments of discouragement. So we get weary and want to quit. That's why the writer of Hebrews told us to get our eyes off our problems, as real as they may be, and consider Jesus. When we reflect on Him, we do not grow weary and lose heart."

He never promised we wouldn't get discouraged, He promised there is joy on the other side.

Have a "consider Him" day today, full of joy.

48

In your struggle against sin, you have not yet resisted to the point of shedding your blood. And have you completely forgotten this word of encouragement that addresses you as a father addresses his son? It says, 'My son, do not make light of the Lord's discipline, and do not lose heart when he rebukes you, because the Lord disciplines the one he loves, and he hastens everyone he accepts as his son.'
Hebrews 12:4-6

I have noticed an inordinate amount of whining and complaining on social media. Don't get me wrong, I understand how life and circumstances can get tough. But beginning Monday with grumbling about your life, your job, and your co-workers and longing for Friday is a sad way to live. God offers so much more.

Living without complaint is all in your perspective. Look for what God can teach you in the difficulties and struggles. Be open to the way He wants to prune and shape your character. When we complain too much about our lot in life, we have "completely forgotten" the word of encouragement from our Father.

He is your Father and He loves you, and anything He permits into your life is for your good: to strengthen you or perhaps to discipline you, but in either case, to demonstrate, in the worst of times, His consuming love for you.

Have a "no complaints" day today.

49

Endure hardship as discipline; God is treating you as his children. For what children are not disciplined by their father? If you are not disciplined—and everyone undergoes discipline—then you are not legitimate, not true sons and daughters at all. Moreover, we have all had human fathers who disciplined us and we respected them for it. How much more should we submit to the Father of spirits and live!
Hebrews 12:7-9

Everyone goes through hard times. It's not a matter of if, but a matter of when. Life is hard. However, if we can view those tough times as God preparing us for this life and the next, it might help us to "run the race." And even in our worst times, we can be encouraged.

When we see our tough times as God's love being poured out on us, we are encouraged. Did your parents ever say something profound just before they spanked you? Something like, "This is for your own good." Or maybe, "This will teach you not to…." Or my all-time favorite, "This is going to hurt me more than it hurts you." I never figured that one out, until I became a parent. Then it became crystal clear. You see, if our parents didn't love us, they would leave us to ourselves, to grow up on our own the best way we could. You wouldn't do that to your children, and God won't allow that with His kids either.

Real living is not the absence of hard times and the Lord's discipline. Real living is rejoicing in the love and presence of God, even during the tough times. His discipline is a mark of His love for us. So thank Him for loving you enough to allow it.

Have a "loving my hardship" day.

50

They disciplined us for a little while as they thought best; but God disciplines us for our good, in order that we may share in his holiness. No discipline seems pleasant at the time, but painful. Later on, however, it produces a harvest of righteousness and peace for those who have been trained by it.
Hebrews 12:10-11

God disciplines us. Our verses today draw a parallel between God our Father and our earthly parents. Here we get a glimpse of one more facet of how God allows uncomfortable things into our lives because they bring a harvest of righteousness and peace. His aim is for us to "share in His holiness."

"Wait a minute. I thought God wanted me to be happy." The U.S. constitution guarantees the pursuit of happiness, but God is far more interested in your holiness. Don't misunderstand. The Lord usually gives you more happiness than you deserve and probably more than you can stand, but along with the gladness, there will be discipline.

He allows some experiences to knock off our rough edges. He helps us get rid of everything that doesn't look like Jesus, as He conforms us to His image.

In C.S. Lewis' children's tale, *The Lion, The Witch, and The Wardrobe*, the children ask the beavers about the lion Aslan (a type of Christ), "Is He safe?"

The beaver answers, "Safe? Who said anything about safe? 'Course he isn't safe. But he's good. He's the King, I tell you."

Does it hurt to receive the Lord's discipline? Of course it hurts. He is God. But it is good for you, I tell you.

Have a "disciplined" day today.

51

Make every effort to live in peace with everyone and to be holy; without holiness no one will see the Lord. See to it that no one falls short of the grace of God and that no bitter root grows up to cause trouble and defile many.
Hebrews 12:14-15

The coffee is on and it is good.

Can you think of someone who ticks you off? I've often said that I could have been a great pastor if it had not been for all of those people I had to deal with. Can I let you in on a big secret? Some people are hard to live with. Can I let you in on another secret? You might have been the person someone else thought of when he or she read that first question.

You are not perfect, and neither are the people around you. That's why it takes an effort to live in peace with people who are less than easy to get along with. They may be in your family or in your church or at your workplace. There's no getting away from them, but the instruction is to make every effort to live in peace with them.

I don't profess to understand it, but somehow your willingness to make every effort to get along is tied to your holiness. Have you quit too soon trying to get along with someone? Every effort is like a chain link to your being holy. Not making an effort provides fertile soil for bitterness to grow and flourish. You've got to go to the garden and pull out the bitter roots.

Have an "every effort" day today.

52

You have not come to a mountain that can be touched and that is burning with fire; to darkness, gloom and storm; to a trumpet blast or to such a voice speaking words that those who heard it begged that no further word be spoken to them, because they could not bear what was commanded: 'If even an animal touches the mountain, it must be stoned to death.' The sight was so terrifying that Moses said, 'I am trembling with fear.' But you have come to Mount Zion, to the city of the living God, the heavenly Jerusalem. You have come to thousands upon thousands of angels in joyful assembly, to the church of the firstborn, whose names are written in heaven. You have come to God, the Judge of all, to the spirits of the righteous made perfect, to Jesus the mediator of a new covenant, and to the sprinkled blood that speaks a better word than the blood of Abel.
Hebrews 12: 18-24

Do you want to go mountain climbing this morning?

We are all climbing a mountain. The question is which mountain are you climbing? When God gave the law to Moses, it was a frightening experience for the people. They even came to the point where they begged that they might not be able to hear God's voice. This giving of the law at Mt. Sinai represented the way of works and sacrifices. This was the Old Covenant. But here God reminds us that the mountain we are climbing is not a frightening one. Ours is not a mountain of laws and works, but a mountain of grace. While the way up the mountain of legalism is hard and scary, with obstacles so severe that no one can successfully climb it, the way up Mount Grace (Zion) has been made smooth and available to everyone through the death of Jesus. That's why He is called the "pioneer", the "trailblazer", the "author" of our faith.

A successful businessman told his pastor as tears formed in his eyes, "I've spent my entire life climbing the ladder of success, only to find out when I reached the top that the ladder is leaning against the wrong wall."

Are you climbing a mountain of fear or a mountain of joy? Are you putting on the boots of legalism or of grace? You climb Mount Fear alone, but Jesus is with you if you choose Mount Grace.

Have a "mountain climbing" day today.

53

Therefore, since we are receiving a kingdom that cannot be shaken, let us be thankful, and so worship God acceptably with reverence and awe, for our "God is a consuming fire."
Hebrews 12:28-29

Has God ever shaken your world?

For some of us, it doesn't take much to shake ours. But I'm asking about really shaking, as in shaking it so bad that some things come tumbling down. One phone call can cause our world to be shaken.

When I received a call that my brother and sister-in-law had just been killed in a car accident, my world was forever changed. One call from a doctor informing you of a cancer diagnosis can turn your world upside down. A shaking can be good or it can be bad, but it's almost always painful.

Sometimes our circumstances can become so harsh, that we are driven to turn to God, rather than rely on our own self-sufficiency. That can be a "good" shaking. The pain gets our attention. You might not know that a bone in your foot was broken and needed attention, if not for the pain. Primarily though, the pain drives us to dependence upon God. God works through the pain of our lives. Someone once said, "It is doubtful that God can use greatly, someone who hasn't hurt deeply."

God, who cannot be shaken, sometimes allows a shaking to occur in our lives so that only those things which cannot be shaken remain. Think about it. What are the things in your life that need to be shaken loose and what things cannot be shaken loose?

Cling to that which is rooted in your relationship with God, hold loosely those things that are centered in you. He has included you in His unshakeable kingdom. Therefore, He deserves our thanks and our worship, and we need to give them, remembering that our God is not only a loving heavenly Father but also a consuming fire. So approach Him with nothing less than reverence and awe.

Have an "unshakeable" day today.

54

Keep on loving one another as brothers and sisters.
Hebrews 13:1

Have you ever noticed how some of the simplest of God's instructions are the most difficult to pull off? We tend to complicate the things of God. Don't misunderstand, the things of God are immense; they are grand; they are intricate; they are difficult to comprehend. But all the bigness, all the complication, all the difficulty is on God's side, not man's. God's practical words to us are really very simple. So while men are digging into the deep things of God and profound theology, God reminds us of the uncomplicated truth: Love each other.

It's that simple. God instructs us to keep on loving one another. And by the way, He is not telling us to do something of which we are incapable. He will love others through you if you will allow Him. He specializes in the simple as well as the complex. Why not start today?

The Lord says, "Keep on" loving each other. That means it is something you do, rather than something you feel. If you try to extend love based on the way you feel, you will never succeed. It is much like the old time steam-driven trains. They had, in this order, an engine, a coal car, passenger or freight cars, and a caboose. The engine supplied the power, the coal car supplied the engine, and the caboose, which had no power, simply trailed along behind. God's love through you is the engine, your faith is the coal car that feeds the engine, and your feelings are the caboose that follows along. The caboose is usually there, but the train can run without it. The feelings of love will usually follow, but His love will flow through you with or without the feelings. So, love with His love and let Him take care of the feelings.

Have a "loving" day today.

55

Do not forget to show hospitality to strangers, for by so doing some people have shown hospitality to angels without knowing it.
Hebrews 13:2

My wife and I operate a bed and breakfast for pastors, church staff, missionaries, and Christian workers at our house. The B&B is called The Creek House. It's free to these men and women because the Lord supplies our needs. Our desire is to give them a place where they can simply relax for a couple of days.

It is easy to show hospitality to those we know, but many of the people who come here are complete strangers. Not knowing the guests makes hospitality a little harder until we remember what hospitality is. Hospitality is the art of making other people feel "at home" in your world. Our purpose is to give them a place to get away and rest from the routine for a couple of days.

People have two basic needs. They need to be loved and they need to be accepted. Our guests come to us from many different backgrounds, cultures, and languages. Sometimes it is a real task to make them feel at home. We decided that the best way to do that was to decrease the expectations. We don't have an agenda for our guests. There is no set schedule of activities. There is no teaching or counseling. The only thing that happens is that we invite them into our world and interact with them at whatever level they want us to. We simply talk with them, or listen to them, or if asked, give a thought or two. We try to make them feel "at home" in our world.

Do you go out of your way to make others feel at home in your world? It can happen anywhere or anytime. The next time you meet someone, try to help him or her feel at ease. And who knows? God may have sent them to you.

The word "angel" means, a messenger. Hope you see a messenger today.

Have a "hospitable" day today.

56

*Keep your lives free from the love of money and
be content with what you have, because God has said,
"Never will I leave you; never will I forsake you."
So we say with confidence, "The Lord is my helper; I
will not be afraid. What can mere mortals do to me?"*
Hebrews 13:5-6

As you sip your cup of coffee this morning, ask yourself, "Am I content?" Are you happy with where you are in your life and what you have? Or do you constantly think about what else you want? The next purchase? The next thing? Or maybe even the next relationship?

Paul said once that he had learned in every circumstance, to be content. (See Philippians 4:11.) Have you learned that lesson yet? It doesn't come easy. I saw a bumper sticker once that read, "The one that dies with the most toys, wins." The slogan isn't true. The one that dies with the most toys leaves all his toys for someone else.

How much stuff do you really need? God is a giver of many gifts and He isn't against stuff. My definition of stuff is anything you can't take to heaven with you. Someone asked once, "How much stuff will God let me have?"

I answered, "As much as you can hold in your hands without clenching your fist around it and calling it yours."

Somehow, we have bought into the lie that a person is not successful unless they have accumulated a lot of wealth. A millionaire was asked, "How much money will it take to satisfy you?" And he said, "The next million." It is always the next million, the next deal, the next rung on the ladder, the next acquisition. The problem is not the wealth itself. The Bible never states that money, in and of itself, is bad. But Paul did say in 1 Timothy 6:10 that, "the love of money is the root of all evil: which while some coveted after, they have erred from the faith, and pierced themselves through with many sorrows."

When I look back on my life, and whether or not I was successful, I don't want to look at bank accounts or possessions. Rather I want to leave a legacy of godly children and grandchildren, and people who were helped somehow by the life I lived and the words I spoke. I could be content with that. Can you?

The Old Testament passage quoted in our verses today actually means, "I will never, no never, no never, leave you or forsake you." God repeats Himself three times. The promise is that you have the Lord—all of Him. And that's enough. Seek to find contentment in Him.

Have a "contented" day today.

57

Jesus Christ is the same yesterday and today and forever. Do not be carried away by all kinds of strange teachings. It is good for our hearts to be strengthened by grace, not by eating ceremonial foods, which is of no benefit to those who do so.
Hebrews 13:8-9

For over forty years of pastoring churches, I have pretty much heard all of the theological and ecclesiastical fads that have come along. I've experienced a little of the "worship wars" over how we should sing and praise the Lord. A new emphasis comes along, as if it has just been discovered. And while I realize that different groups of Christians will emphasize different truths, at different times, folks remember: There really is nothing new under the sun.

We must keep our eyes on Jesus. Music styles come and go. Emphases ebb and flow. While everything around us is changing, Jesus, Himself is constant. He never changes. His love never changes for you. He loved you as much when you were a child as He does right now. His love for you hasn't grown with your maturity. Although you have changed, His love for you hasn't.

He still views sin today the way He did when He died on the cross for you. You won't hear the Lord say, "Well, the culture has changed. Things are different now. I guess I will have to re-evaluate how I look at sin." No, because He does not change. Some people say that God is different in the Old Testament from the New Testament. No, He is the same. One of the attributes of God is He doesn't change.

Have a "He's the same" day today.

58

Do not be carried away by all kinds of strange teachings. It is good for our hearts to be strengthened by grace, not by eating ceremonial foods, which is of no benefit to those who do so.
Hebrews 13:9

Have you ever noticed how easy it is to get sidetracked when it comes to the truths of God?

Many denominations and movements have been started by men who camped out on one bad interpretation of one or two Scriptures. I'm amazed at how many "new" truths are discovered every day. Here's a suggestion for you to consider. If it's true, then it's not new. If it's new, then it's not true. God is not introducing new truth to a housewife standing at her kitchen sink or a great orator counting the money he has made from sending out prayer cloths. God doesn't change. Jesus is the same yesterday and today and forever, remember? Therefore, His truth is unchanging.

God gave us truth when He gave us His Word. Stay with that. Focus on the main thing. It is His truth that will set you free. Let God speak truth to you through His Word.

And don't forget, grace is the foundation for our relationship with Him, not ritual or ceremony. Chasing strange teachings, new truth, or ceremonies in order to be approved or accepted by God will wear you out. Living in grace will give you strength and rest.

Have a "strengthened" day today.

59

For here we do not have an enduring city, but we are looking for the city that is to come.
Hebrews 13:14

Isn't it amazing that men build cities, thinking they will last forever?

The moment a building is completed, it has already started to decay. Everything is in the process of falling apart. All you have to do is visit the ruins of Rome and visit the Coliseum to see that things are passing away. Or visit the Parthenon in Greece. Or any number of ruins scattered throughout the world. Or if that is too much of a trip for you, go find an old barn that is rotting away, and remember that it was once new. Whether it's the grandest architectural wonder or a humble barn, every building eventually decays.

The only thing that is eternal is that which we cannot see. The scary thing is that what is true of inanimate objects is even more true of man. We are in the process of passing away.

I'm hearing more and more of my peers who have become terribly sick and have died, it seems to me, much too young. It's both tragic and a bit ironic that we focus most of our energy on the things that are crumbling.

Enjoy your life, and enjoy your stuff, but keep your eyes on the enduring city to come, not the one you're living in now.

Have a "looking for that city" day today.

60

Through Jesus, therefore, let us continually offer to God a sacrifice of praise—the fruit of lips that openly profess his name.
Hebrews 13:15

Hope your day is off to a good start.

This may be one of those "shotgun" thoughts this morning. In other words, there are several thoughts in verse fifteen.

First, our praise to God can come only through Jesus. God does not accept praise apart from a relationship with Jesus Christ. Why? Because Jesus said, "I am the way, the truth, and the life. No man comes to the Father except through me" (John 14:6)."

Second, our praise should be continuous. In other words, we should have an attitude of praise.

Next, our praise will sometimes cost us something. It is called a "sacrifice of praise." When we are going through tough times, it is hard to praise God. But we praise Him anyway as an offering.

And our praise should be professed openly to God. We hear so many people say that our faith is a private thing. Let me say something very profound. That is hogwash. The Word of God plainly states that praise and testimony are to be public.

There is a need and a time for a closet of prayer, but the giving of praise openly is the natural, normal, reasonable fruit of our lips because our hearts are full.

Have a "praising" day today.

61

*And do not forget to do good and to share with
others, for with such sacrifices God is pleased.*
Hebrews 13:16

Occasionally someone will say, "I want the deep things of God."

We talk about deep truth as if we would walk in it, if we could just hear it. The problem is that the deep things of God are sometimes right there on the surface. Read today's verse again, "And do not forget to do good and to share with others, for with such sacrifices God is pleased." It is so simple yet extremely deep and profound.

Don't forget to do good, do the right thing, and be sure to share with others. And with those simple deeds, you will please God.

Pleasing God is not necessarily about the modified, historical, eschatological, dualism that is revealed in the kingdom model of the incarnation. Who would have thought that doing good and sharing would be deeper than gathering around the toes on the beast of prophecy? Go figure. And go do good.

Have a "deeper" day today.

Coffee and Life:

One sip at a time.

62

Now may the God of peace, who through the blood of the eternal covenant brought back from the dead our Lord Jesus, that great Shepherd of the sheep, equip you with everything good for doing his will, and may he work in us what is pleasing to him, through Jesus Christ, to whom be glory for ever and ever. Amen.
Hebrews 13:20-21

The writer of Hebrews concludes with a prayer. In this prayer for the Hebrew people, he explained how God, who gave us Jesus Christ as the full payment for our sin, equips us to do what He has called us to do. We don't have to depend on our strength to pull it off. Every demand God makes upon us is actually a demand on the Christ who lives in us.

He lives in us and He lives through us. Throughout the entire book of Hebrews we have seen the One who is above the angels, higher than a high priest, greater than Moses, better than the Tabernacle, stronger than the sacrificial system, and more wonderful than the old covenant. He redeemed us with His blood, and in Him, all the Old Testament figures placed their faith. He is the One who lives in you.

He will never, no never, no never leave you nor forsake you. He equips you to do His will and actually works through you to do it. All these things bring Him glory.

Have a "glorious" day today.

ABOUT THE AUTHOR

Dick Sisk is the pastor of Tarpley Baptist Church in the beautiful Hill Country of Texas. He and his wife Barbara have four daughters and nine grandchildren.

Dick is an alumni of Jacksonville College, Texas Tech University, and holds a Master's degree in Biblical Studies from Criswell College as well as a Master of Divinity and Doctor of Ministry from Southwestern Baptist Theological Seminary.

Dick developed a men's program and ministry for the Memphis Cancer Foundation and served as Vice-President/General Manager of Turpin Meadow Guest Ranch in Jackson Hole, Wyoming, and has been involved in Southern Baptist ministries such as the International Mission Board. Dick served as a chaplain for football teams for nearly forty years including 12 years as chaplain of the University of Memphis football team.

His greatest love is spending time with his wife, children, and grandchildren. Dick is an avid outdoorsman with a passion for big-game hunting, fishing, and golf. He also enjoys woodworking, music, and song writing.

Follow Doc on Facebook:
dick.sisk

Follow The Creek House on Facebook:
The-Creek-House

Doc would love to hear from you. Email:
flatgap73@yahoo.com

Made in the USA
Lexington, KY
18 June 2013